Mastering Money: A Guicy
for College

Helena Johansson

Copyright © [2023]

Title: Mastering Money: A Guide to Financial Literacy for College Students

Author: Helena Johansson

This book was printed and published by [Publisher's Helena Johansson] in [2023]

ISBN:

TABLE OF CONTENTS

Chapter 4: Investing for the Future   32

Introduction to Investing

Types of Investments

Risk and Return

Building an Investment Portfolio

Chapter 5: Navigating the Job Market   41

Resume Writing Tips

Job Search Strategies

Interview Preparation

Negotiating Job Offers

Chapter 6: Entrepreneurship and Side Hustles 49

Exploring Entrepreneurship

Identifying Business Opportunities

Developing a Business Plan

Managing Finances as an Entrepreneur

Chapter 7: Insurance and Risk Management

Understanding Insurance Policies

Health Insurance Options

Renters and Auto Insurance

Protecting Your Financial Future

Chapter 8: Smart Consumerism

Comparison Shopping

Understanding Consumer Rights

Avoiding Identity Theft

Making Informed Financial Decisions

Chapter 9: Financial Independence and Future Planning

Building an Emergency Fund

Retirement Planning for Students

Estate Planning Basics

Long-Term Financial Goals

Chapter 1: Understanding Financial Basics

Importance of Financial Literacy

In today's society, financial literacy has become an essential skill for success. As college students, you are embarking on a new phase of life where financial decisions and responsibilities will play a significant role. Understanding the importance of financial literacy will not only help you navigate through your college years but also set you on the path to financial success in the future.

One of the primary reasons financial literacy is crucial is because it empowers you to make informed decisions about your money. By acquiring the necessary knowledge and skills, you can effectively manage your finances, avoid debt, and secure a stable financial future. Financial literacy enables you to understand concepts such as budgeting, saving, investing, and credit, which are fundamental aspects of personal finance.

Developing financial literacy skills also provides you with a sense of control and independence. It allows you to take charge of your financial decisions, rather than relying on others to manage your money. By learning how to budget effectively, you can allocate your funds towards essentials, savings, and even leisure activities, ensuring a healthy balance between spending and saving.

Furthermore, financial literacy equips you with the skills to plan for your future. By understanding the importance of saving and investing early on, you can start building a solid financial foundation. Learning about long-term financial goals, such as retirement planning and homeownership, becomes crucial as you transition into adulthood. With proper financial literacy, you can make informed decisions that will benefit you in the long run.

Financial literacy also plays a vital role in reducing financial stress. College students often face financial challenges, such as student loan debt and limited income. However, having a strong understanding of personal finance can help alleviate some of these stressors. With the knowledge and skills to manage your money effectively, you can make smart financial decisions that minimize debt and maximize your financial well-being.

In conclusion, financial literacy is of utmost importance for college students aiming for success. It empowers you to make informed decisions, take control of your financial future, and reduce financial stress. By mastering the principles of personal finance, you can build a solid foundation for a prosperous life. Remember, financial literacy is not an option but a necessity on your journey towards financial success.

Setting Financial Goals

One of the key ingredients for achieving financial success is setting clear and achievable financial goals. In this subchapter, we will explore the importance of setting financial goals and provide practical tips to help you define and attain your desired financial outcomes.

Why Set Financial Goals?

Setting financial goals is crucial because it provides direction and purpose to your financial decisions. Without clear goals, it is easy to drift aimlessly and make haphazard financial choices that can hinder your progress towards success. By setting goals, you can prioritize your spending, saving, and investing habits to align with your long-term objectives.

Defining Your Financial Goals

To begin, take some time to reflect on what financial success means to you. Consider both short-term and long-term objectives. Short-term goals may include saving for an emergency fund, paying off student loans, or purchasing a new laptop. Long-term goals may involve saving for retirement, buying a house, or starting a business. It is essential to set goals that are specific, measurable, achievable, relevant, and time-bound (SMART goals). This framework ensures that your goals are clear, trackable, and realistic.

Creating an Action Plan

Once you have identified your financial goals, it is time to develop an action plan to reach them. Break down your goals into smaller, manageable steps. For instance, if your goal is to save $10,000 for a down payment on a house within three years, calculate how much you need to save each month to reach that target. Consider adjusting your spending habits, exploring additional income opportunities, or seeking financial advice to help you stay on track.

Tracking Your Progress

Regularly monitoring your progress is crucial for staying motivated and making adjustments when necessary. Set up a system to track your income, expenses, and savings. This can be as simple as using a spreadsheet or utilizing personal finance apps. Review your progress periodically and make any necessary revisions to your action plan.

In conclusion, setting financial goals is a fundamental step towards achieving financial success. By defining your objectives, creating an action plan, and monitoring your progress, you can take control of your financial future and make informed decisions that will lead you to financial prosperity. Remember, it's never too early to start setting financial goals, so get started today!

Budgeting 101

Budgeting 101: The Key to Financial Success

Introduction:

Welcome to "Budgeting 101," a subchapter of the book "Mastering Money: A Guide to Financial Literacy for College Students." In this chapter, we will delve into the essential skill of budgeting and how it can pave the way for your financial success. As a student, mastering the art of budgeting will not only help you manage your money effectively but also set the foundation for a successful future. So, let's dive in and discover the key principles of budgeting!

Understanding Budgeting:

Budgeting is the process of creating a plan for your money, ensuring that you spend it wisely and achieve your financial goals. It involves tracking your income, setting aside money for essential expenses, saving for the future, and managing discretionary spending. By developing a budget, you gain control over your finances, avoid unnecessary debt, and create a solid financial foundation.

Creating a Budget:

To create an effective budget, start by understanding your income sources and regular expenses. Identify your fixed expenses, such as rent, tuition fees, and utilities, and allocate a portion of your income to cover them. Then, set aside a percentage for savings and emergency funds. The remaining amount can be utilized for discretionary spending, including entertainment, dining out, and shopping.

Remember, it's crucial to strike a balance between saving and enjoying your college experience.

Tracking Your Expenses:

Tracking your expenses is a fundamental aspect of budgeting. By monitoring your spending habits, you can identify areas where you can cut back and save more. Utilize budgeting apps or spreadsheets to record your expenses, categorize them, and compare them against your budget. This practice will help you stay on track and make adjustments as necessary.

Adapting to Financial Changes:

As a college student, your financial situation will constantly evolve. Part-time jobs, internships, scholarships, or financial aid can significantly impact your income. Therefore, it's essential to review and adjust your budget regularly to reflect these changes accurately. Be prepared to adapt and make necessary modifications to your spending plan.

Benefits of Budgeting:

Budgeting offers numerous benefits beyond financial management. It instills discipline, promotes responsible money habits, and reduces stress associated with financial uncertainty. Moreover, budgeting allows you to work towards your long-term goals, such as saving for a study abroad program, paying off student loans, or investing in your future.

Conclusion:

Congratulations on taking the first step towards financial success by delving into the world of budgeting! By implementing the principles outlined in this subchapter, you can develop a strong foundation for managing your money effectively. Remember, budgeting is not about restricting your spending; it's about making informed choices and aligning your financial decisions with your goals. Start budgeting today and pave the way for a prosperous future!

Creating a Personal Spending Plan

In today's fast-paced world, managing your money effectively is crucial for achieving financial success. As a college student, it is essential to develop healthy financial habits that will set you up for a secure future. This subchapter aims to guide you in creating a personal spending plan that will help you make informed decisions about your finances.

A personal spending plan is a detailed budget that outlines your income, expenses, and financial goals. It serves as a roadmap to track your spending, save money, and avoid unnecessary debt. Here are some steps to help you create a solid spending plan:

1. Assess Your Income: Start by calculating your sources of income, such as part-time jobs, scholarships, or allowances. Determine the amount you receive regularly and establish a realistic monthly income.

2. Track Your Expenses: Keep a record of all your expenses for a month. Categorize them into essential needs like rent, groceries, and transportation, and discretionary expenses like entertainment and dining out. This will give you a clear picture of where your money is going.

3. Set Financial Goals: Define short-term and long-term financial goals. Short-term goals can include saving for a new laptop or a vacation, while long-term goals may involve paying off student loans or saving for retirement. Having clear objectives will help you stay motivated and focused on your spending plan.

4. Create a Budget: Based on your income and expenses, create a monthly budget that aligns with your goals. Allocate a specific amount for each category, ensuring your income covers all your expenses while leaving room for savings.

5. Monitor and Adjust: Regularly review your spending plan to track your progress. Keep an eye on any deviations and make adjustments if necessary. Be flexible with your budget but stay committed to your financial goals.

6. Seek Financial Advice: If you find it challenging to create a spending plan, don't hesitate to seek guidance from financial advisors or mentors. They can provide valuable insights and help tailor a plan to your specific needs.

Remember, mastering money is a lifelong journey, and developing good financial habits as a student will set you on the path to success. By creating a personal spending plan, you will gain control over your finances, reduce stress, and pave the way for a prosperous future. Start today and take charge of your financial well-being!

Chapter 2: Managing Your Money

Tracking Expenses

One of the most important skills you can develop as a college student is the ability to track your expenses. It is crucial to have a clear understanding of where your money is going in order to achieve financial success. By diligently monitoring your expenses, you can make informed decisions about your spending habits and ensure that you are on the right track towards your financial goals.

Tracking expenses allows you to gain control over your finances. It provides you with an accurate picture of your spending patterns and helps identify areas where you can cut back or make adjustments. It is easy to lose track of small daily expenses, but over time, they can add up and have a significant impact on your overall budget. By keeping track of every dollar you spend, you will be able to see exactly where your money is going and make necessary adjustments in your spending habits.

There are several methods you can use to track your expenses. One popular approach is to maintain a detailed spreadsheet or use budgeting software that allows you to categorize your expenses. This method gives you a clear overview of your spending in different categories such as groceries, entertainment, transportation, and more. It enables you to see how much you are spending in each category and identify any areas where you may be overspending.

Another effective way to track expenses is by using mobile apps specifically designed for this purpose. These apps allow you to easily enter your expenses on the go and provide real-time updates on your spending. Some apps even offer features like setting spending limits, sending notifications when you exceed your budget, and generating reports to analyze your spending patterns.

Remember, tracking expenses is not meant to restrict your spending but rather to empower you to make informed financial decisions. It helps you prioritize your expenses and allocate your money towards things that truly matter to you. By tracking your expenses, you will be able to identify where you can save money, make adjustments to your spending habits, and ultimately achieve financial success.

In conclusion, tracking your expenses is a crucial skill that every college student must master. It allows you to have a clear understanding of your spending habits and make informed decisions about your finances. By using methods such as detailed spreadsheets or mobile apps, you can easily track your expenses and identify areas where you can make adjustments. Remember, tracking expenses is not about restricting your spending but rather about empowering yourself to achieve financial success. Start tracking your expenses today, and take control of your financial future.

Saving Strategies

One of the fundamental aspects of achieving financial success is developing effective saving strategies. As college students, it is crucial to understand the importance of saving money and how it can contribute to your long-term financial well-being. In this section, we will explore various saving strategies that will help you make the most out of your college experience and set you up for financial success in the future.

1. Set Clear Financial Goals: Start by setting clear and achievable financial goals. Whether it's saving for a study abroad program, buying a car, or paying off student loans, having specific goals will help you stay motivated and focused on your saving efforts.

2. Create a Budget: Develop a budget that accounts for your income and expenses. Track your spending and identify areas where you can cut back. By allocating a portion of your income towards savings, you can build a financial cushion for unexpected expenses and future investments.

3. Embrace Frugality: Embracing a frugal lifestyle can significantly impact your savings. Look for ways to reduce expenses, such as cooking meals at home, using student discounts, and buying used textbooks. Small changes in your spending habits can add up to substantial savings over time.

4. Automate Savings: Take advantage of technology by setting up automatic transfers from your checking account to a separate savings account. By automating your savings, you can ensure that a portion of

your income goes directly into savings before you have a chance to spend it.

5. Take Advantage of Student Discounts: Many businesses offer discounts exclusively for students. Always carry your student ID and inquire about discounts wherever you go. These savings may seem small individually but can accumulate over time.

6. Avoid Impulsive Purchases: Before making a purchase, pause and ask yourself if it aligns with your financial goals. Avoid impulsive buying decisions and give yourself time to evaluate whether it's a necessity or a want. Delaying gratification can help you save money and make more informed financial choices.

7. Start an Emergency Fund: It's essential to have an emergency fund to cover unexpected expenses like medical bills, car repairs, or sudden job loss. Aim to save three to six months' worth of living expenses in a separate account to provide financial security in times of crisis.

By implementing these saving strategies, you will not only develop healthy financial habits but also gain peace of mind. Remember, successful money management during your college years can set the stage for a financially secure future. Start saving now, and you'll reap the benefits for years to come.

Paying Off Student Loans

One of the most significant financial challenges that college students face is paying off their student loans. As you embark on your journey to financial independence, it is crucial to develop a solid plan to tackle this debt and set yourself up for success. In this subchapter, we will explore strategies and tips on how to effectively pay off your student loans and achieve financial freedom.

1. Understand Your Loans: Start by familiarizing yourself with the terms and conditions of your student loans. Take note of the interest rates, repayment options, and any potential grace periods. This knowledge will help you make informed decisions when it comes to paying off your debt.

2. Create a Budget: Developing a budget is essential for managing your finances, including your student loan payments. Determine your income, expenses, and allocate a portion of your budget towards loan repayment. By tracking your spending and cutting unnecessary expenses, you can free up more money to put towards your loans.

3. Make Extra Payments: Whenever possible, aim to make extra payments towards your student loans. Even small additional payments can significantly reduce the overall interest you pay over time. Consider using any windfalls, such as tax refunds or bonuses, to make extra payments and accelerate your debt repayment.

4. Explore Loan Forgiveness Programs: Investigate if you qualify for any loan forgiveness programs. Some professions, such as teaching or public service, offer loan forgiveness options for those who meet

specific criteria. Research and take advantage of these programs to potentially eliminate a portion of your debt.

5. Consider Refinancing: If you have multiple student loans with varying interest rates, refinancing may be a valuable option. By consolidating your loans into one, you may secure a lower interest rate and simplify your repayment process. However, carefully evaluate the terms and conditions of refinancing before making a decision.

6. Seek Professional Assistance: If you find yourself overwhelmed or unsure about your loan repayment strategy, consider seeking help from a financial advisor or student loan counselor. These professionals can provide personalized guidance and help you navigate the complexities of paying off your student loans.

Remember, paying off your student loans requires discipline and perseverance. Be patient with yourself and stay committed to your financial goals. By implementing these strategies and taking control of your debt, you can pave the way for financial success and a brighter future.

Building Credit History

In today's world, having a solid credit history is crucial for financial success. Whether you plan on buying a car, renting an apartment, or even starting your own business, your credit history will play a significant role in determining your eligibility and the terms you'll receive. This subchapter aims to provide college students with insights and strategies for building a strong credit history, laying the foundation for a prosperous financial future.

1.   Understanding   Credit:
To begin, it's essential to understand what credit is and how it works. Credit is essentially borrowed money that you can use to make purchases, with the promise to repay it later, usually with interest. Building credit involves responsibly using credit cards, loans, and other forms of credit, while making timely payments and maintaining a low debt-to-credit ratio.

2.   Start   Small:
For students who have yet to establish credit, starting small is key. Consider applying for a student credit card or a secured credit card that requires a cash deposit as collateral. These cards typically have lower credit limits, making it easier to manage and build credit responsibly. Use them for small purchases and be sure to pay off the balance in full each month.

3.   Pay   Bills   on   Time:
One of the most critical factors in building credit history is making timely payments. Late payments can have a significant negative impact on your credit score. Create a budget and set reminders to ensure you

never miss a payment. Consider setting up automatic payments or electronic reminders to stay on track.

4.   Keep   Credit   Utilization   Low: Credit utilization refers to the percentage of your available credit that you're using. Keeping this ratio low can positively impact your credit score. Aim to keep your credit utilization below 30% by paying off balances consistently and refraining from maxing out credit cards.

5.   Diversify   Your   Credit   Mix: Having a diverse mix of credit accounts can demonstrate responsible credit management. Consider opening a small installment loan, such as a student loan or a car loan, in addition to using credit cards. However, be cautious not to take on excessive debt or open multiple accounts at once, as this can have a negative impact.

6.   Monitor   Your   Credit: Regularly monitoring your credit is essential to identify and address any errors or fraudulent activity. Obtain a free copy of your credit report annually from each of the three major credit bureaus and review it for accuracy. Additionally, consider signing up for a credit monitoring service that alerts you to any changes or suspicious activity.

Building credit history is a gradual process that requires patience and responsible financial habits. By starting early and following these guidelines, students can establish a strong credit foundation that will open doors to financial opportunities and success in the future. Remember, building credit is not about accumulating debt; it's about demonstrating responsible borrowing and repayment behavior.

Chapter 3: Banking and Financial Services

Choosing a Bank Account

In today's fast-paced world, managing your money effectively is crucial for achieving success. As college students, it's essential to develop good financial habits early on. One crucial step towards financial literacy is choosing the right bank account. In this subchapter, we will explore the key factors to consider when selecting a bank account that aligns with your goals and maximizes your chances of financial success.

1. Types of Bank Accounts: Before choosing a bank account, it's important to understand the different types available. The most common types include checking accounts, savings accounts, and money market accounts. Each type serves a specific purpose, so evaluate your needs and select accordingly.

2. Fees and Charges: Banks may impose various fees on their accounts, such as monthly maintenance fees, overdraft fees, or ATM fees. As a student, you should prioritize accounts that offer fee waivers or low charges, allowing you to keep more of your hard-earned money.

3. Interest Rates: Interest rates determine how much money your account will earn over time. Look for accounts that offer competitive interest rates, especially for savings accounts or money market accounts. Higher interest rates can help your money grow faster and provide a solid foundation for your financial future.

4. Accessibility and Convenience: Consider the bank's accessibility and convenience, such as the number of branches and ATMs available.

Look for banks that have a strong online banking platform, mobile apps, and offer free online bill payment services. These features will make managing your finances easier and more efficient.

5. Additional Services: Some banks offer additional services like student loans, credit cards, or financial education resources. Choosing a bank that provides such services can be beneficial, especially if you plan to explore these financial avenues during your college journey.

6. Customer Service: Good customer service is crucial when it comes to banking. Research reviews or speak to current customers to determine the bank's reputation for responsiveness, helpfulness, and problem-solving. A bank with excellent customer service can provide peace of mind and ensure you have a smooth banking experience.

Remember, choosing a bank account is a personal decision, and what works for one student may not work for another. Take your time to evaluate your needs, compare different banks, and make an informed choice. By selecting the right bank account, you will set yourself up for financial success and gain valuable skills that will benefit you throughout your college years and beyond.

Understanding Debit and Credit Cards

In today's digital age, where financial transactions are increasingly moving away from cash, it is essential for college students to have a solid understanding of debit and credit cards. These cards have become an integral part of our financial lives, offering convenience, security, and numerous benefits. However, misusing them can lead to financial pitfalls that can hinder your path to success. In this subchapter, we will dive deep into the world of debit and credit cards, equipping you with the knowledge to make informed decisions and harness the power of these tools for your financial well-being.

Firstly, let's differentiate between debit and credit cards. Debit cards are directly linked to your bank account and allow you to spend the money you already have. They are convenient for everyday transactions, ensuring that you only spend what you can afford. On the other hand, credit cards provide you with a line of credit, allowing you to borrow money up to a certain limit. It is crucial to understand that credit cards involve borrowing money that you will need to repay, usually with interest.

In this subchapter, we will explore the benefits and risks associated with both types of cards. Debit cards provide ease of access, budgeting capabilities, and protection against fraudulent charges. However, they may lack the benefits and rewards associated with credit cards, such as cashback, travel rewards, and building credit history. Credit cards, when used responsibly, can offer advantages like building a credit score, purchase protection, and additional financial flexibility. However, they also come with the temptation to overspend and accumulate debt if not managed wisely.

We will delve into important concepts, such as understanding credit card interest rates, fees, and how to choose the right card for your needs. We will discuss responsible credit card usage, including tips on how to avoid debt traps, pay your bills on time, and build a positive credit history.

By the end of this subchapter, you will have a comprehensive understanding of debit and credit cards, empowering you to make financial decisions that align with your goals. Whether it be managing your day-to-day expenses with a debit card or utilizing credit cards to your advantage, mastering these tools will contribute to your financial success. Remember, financial literacy is a journey, and by equipping yourself with knowledge, you are setting yourself up for a prosperous future.

Online and Mobile Banking

In today's digital age, financial transactions have become more convenient and accessible than ever before. Thanks to advancements in technology, students can now take advantage of online and mobile banking services to manage their money efficiently. This subchapter will delve into the world of online and mobile banking, discussing the benefits, features, and potential risks associated with these platforms.

Online banking refers to the ability to access and manage your bank accounts through a secure website or app. With just a few clicks, students can check their account balances, review transaction history, transfer funds between accounts, pay bills, and even deposit checks without ever setting foot in a physical bank branch. The convenience and time-saving nature of online banking make it an excellent tool for busy college students who are always on the go.

Mobile banking takes convenience to the next level by allowing users to perform financial transactions on their smartphones or other portable devices. Through dedicated banking apps, students can access the same features available on online banking platforms, but with the added advantage of mobility. Whether you need to transfer money to a friend, monitor your spending, or receive real-time alerts about your account activity, mobile banking puts the power of financial management right at your fingertips.

One of the significant benefits of online and mobile banking is the ability to track your spending and budget effectively. By regularly reviewing your transaction history and categorizing your expenses, you can gain a comprehensive understanding of where your money is going. Armed with this knowledge, you can make informed decisions about your spending habits and identify areas where you can cut back to achieve financial success.

However, it's essential to be aware of the potential risks associated with online and mobile banking. While banks have implemented stringent security measures, it is still crucial to protect your personal information and maintain strong passwords to prevent unauthorized access to your accounts. Additionally, you should only use secure Wi-Fi networks when accessing your banking information to avoid potential hacking attempts.

In conclusion, online and mobile banking are powerful tools that can help students effectively manage their finances. By taking advantage of these platforms, you can track your spending, create budgets, and make informed financial decisions. However, it is crucial to remain vigilant and protect your personal information to ensure the security of your accounts. With the right precautions, online and mobile banking can be valuable resources on your path to financial success.

Managing Bank Fees

In today's fast-paced world, managing your money is more important than ever. As college students, you are embarking on an exciting journey towards independence and success. One crucial aspect of financial literacy that cannot be overlooked is understanding and effectively managing bank fees.

Banks offer a plethora of services to make your financial life easier, but these conveniences often come at a cost. Bank fees can quickly eat away at your hard-earned money if you're not careful. Therefore, it's essential to equip yourself with the knowledge and strategies necessary to minimize these fees and maximize your financial success.

First and foremost, familiarize yourself with the various types of bank fees. Common fees include monthly maintenance fees, overdraft fees, ATM fees, and foreign transaction fees. Understanding these fees will help you identify potential pitfalls and make informed decisions about your banking activities.

One of the simplest ways to avoid bank fees is to choose a bank that offers fee-free or low-fee accounts specifically designed for students. Many financial institutions have recognized the importance of catering to the unique needs of college students and offer accounts with reduced fees or waived service charges. Take the time to research and compare different banks to find one that aligns with your financial goals.

Maintaining a healthy account balance is another effective strategy to avoid unnecessary fees. Many banks require a minimum balance to waive monthly maintenance fees. By diligently monitoring your account and ensuring it stays above this threshold, you can avoid these charges altogether.

Overdraft fees can be particularly burdensome for students. To avoid them, track your spending diligently and always keep a buffer amount in your account. Consider setting up email or text alerts that notify you when your balance falls below a certain level. This will help you stay proactive in managing your finances and avoid costly overdraft fees.

Lastly, be cautious when using ATMs. While they offer convenience, many banks charge fees for using out-of-network ATMs. To minimize this expense, opt for ATMs that belong to your bank's network. Additionally, plan ahead and withdraw cash in larger amounts less frequently, rather than making multiple small withdrawals that incur multiple fees.

In conclusion, managing bank fees is an essential aspect of financial literacy for college students. By understanding the different types of fees, choosing the right bank, maintaining a healthy account balance, and being mindful of ATM usage, you can minimize fees and maximize your financial success. By mastering this aspect of money management, you are taking a significant step towards a secure and prosperous future.

Chapter 4: Investing for the Future

Introduction to Investing

Investing is a crucial aspect of personal finance that can pave the way for long-term financial success. As a college student, it is never too early to start learning about investing and how it can help you achieve your financial goals. This subchapter aims to provide you with a comprehensive introduction to investing, ensuring that you have the necessary knowledge and skills to make informed investment decisions.

Understanding the Basics: Investing refers to the process of allocating money or resources with the expectation of generating profit or income over time. It involves purchasing assets such as stocks, bonds, real estate, or mutual funds, with the goal of increasing wealth or achieving specific financial objectives. Before diving into the world of investing, it is essential to grasp the fundamental concepts and terminology involved. This chapter will take you through the basics, including risk and return, diversification, asset classes, and investment vehicles.

Setting Financial Goals: To begin your investment journey, it is crucial to establish clear and realistic financial goals. These goals will serve as your roadmap and guide your investment decisions. Whether you aim to save for a down payment on a house, pay off student loans, or build a retirement fund, having specific goals will help you tailor your investment strategy accordingly. This subchapter will discuss the importance of setting financial goals and provide guidance on creating SMART (Specific, Measurable, Achievable, Relevant, and Time-bound) goals.

Understanding   Risk   and   Return:
Investing inherently involves risk, and it is crucial to understand the relationship between risk and return. Higher-risk investments typically offer the potential for higher returns, but also come with a greater chance of losses. This subchapter will explain the concept of risk tolerance and help you assess your own risk tolerance level. It will also cover various investment vehicles, ranging from low-risk to high-risk options, allowing you to make informed decisions based on your risk tolerance and financial goals.

Investment   Strategies:
Having a well-defined investment strategy is essential for successful investing. This subchapter will introduce you to various investment strategies, such as long-term investing, value investing, and dollar-cost averaging. It will explore the advantages and disadvantages of each strategy, helping you determine which approach aligns best with your financial goals and risk tolerance.

By delving into the world of investing, you are taking a crucial step towards financial literacy and securing your future success. This subchapter will equip you with the necessary knowledge and tools to make confident investment decisions and maximize your financial potential. Remember, investing is a long-term commitment, and patience, discipline, and continuous learning are key to achieving your financial goals.

Types of Investments

Investing is an essential aspect of achieving financial success, and understanding different types of investments is crucial for college students who aspire to build wealth and secure their future. This subchapter aims to provide a comprehensive overview of various investment options available to students, helping them make informed decisions and maximize their financial potential.

1. Stocks: Investing in stocks grants you ownership in a company and allows you to benefit from its growth and profitability. Stocks offer potential high returns but also come with a certain level of risk. It is important to conduct thorough research and diversify your portfolio to minimize risks.

2. Bonds: Bonds are fixed-income securities issued by companies or governments to raise capital. They provide a fixed interest rate over a specified period, making them a more stable investment option. Bonds are ideal for conservative investors or those seeking a regular income stream.

3. Mutual Funds: Mutual funds pool money from multiple investors to invest in a diversified portfolio of stocks, bonds, or other securities. They are managed by professionals and offer diversification, making them suitable for beginners. However, it is crucial to analyze the fund's performance and fees before investing.

4. Real Estate: Investing in real estate involves purchasing properties with the aim of generating income or gaining appreciation. Real estate investments can provide a steady cash flow through rental income and

potential tax benefits. However, it requires careful research, knowledge of the market, and significant capital.

5. Exchange-Traded Funds (ETFs): ETFs are similar to mutual funds but trade on stock exchanges. They offer diversification and liquidity while tracking specific market indexes. ETFs often have lower expense ratios compared to mutual funds, making them an attractive investment choice for students.

6. Commodities: Commodities include physical goods such as gold, oil, or agricultural products. Investing in commodities can be done through futures contracts or exchange-traded funds. They serve as a hedge against inflation and offer diversification benefits, but they can be volatile and require extensive research.

7. Options and Futures: Options and futures are derivatives contracts that allow investors to speculate on the future price movements of assets or commodities. While they can provide significant returns, they are highly complex and risky, requiring advanced knowledge and expertise.

As a student, it is important to consider your risk tolerance, investment goals, and time horizon before choosing an investment option. Diversification and regular monitoring of your investments are key to achieving financial success. Consult with a financial advisor or utilize online resources to gain a deeper understanding of these investment types and their suitability for your specific circumstances.

Remember, investing should be viewed as a long-term strategy, and patience, discipline, and continuous learning will help you navigate the ever-changing financial landscape and pave the way for a successful and prosperous future.

Risk and Return

In the world of finance, the concepts of risk and return are fundamental to understanding how to make smart financial decisions. As college students embarking on your journey towards financial success, it is crucial to grasp these concepts and apply them to your own money management strategies. This subchapter will delve into the relationship between risk and return, helping you navigate the complex world of investments and make informed choices.

When it comes to investing, risk and return go hand in hand. Simply put, the potential for higher returns often comes with higher levels of risk. This is because investments that offer greater returns are typically associated with greater uncertainty and volatility. It is essential for you, as students, to recognize this trade-off and make informed decisions that align with your financial goals and risk tolerance.

Understanding risk is the first step towards managing it effectively. Different types of investments carry different levels of risk. Stocks, for instance, are known for their volatile nature and can experience significant fluctuations in value. On the other hand, bonds tend to offer more stable returns but with lower potential for growth. Diversification, or spreading your investments across different asset classes, is a strategy that can help mitigate risk by reducing the impact of any single investment's poor performance.

Return, on the other hand, refers to the profits or gains generated from an investment. It is crucial to assess both the potential return and the accompanying risk before committing your hard-earned money. Remember, higher returns often demand a longer investment horizon and a higher tolerance for risk. As students, you have a unique advantage of time on your side, allowing you to take on more risk in pursuit of higher returns, as you have a longer time frame to recover from any potential losses.

To strike a balance between risk and return, it is essential to clearly define your financial goals and risk tolerance. Are you saving for a short-term goal, such as purchasing a car, or are you investing for the long-term, such as retirement? Knowing your goals will help determine the appropriate level of risk you can afford to take.

Lastly, always conduct thorough research and analysis before making any investment decisions. Educate yourself about different investment options, assess their historical performance, and seek advice from qualified professionals. By understanding the relationship between risk and return, you can make informed financial decisions that align with your aspirations for success.

In conclusion, risk and return are integral components of financial literacy. As college students, it is essential to grasp these concepts to make wise investment choices. By understanding the trade-off between risk and potential return, defining your financial goals, and conducting thorough research, you can navigate the world of investments with confidence and pave the way for a successful financial future.

Building an Investment Portfolio

Investing can be a powerful tool for achieving financial success. By building an investment portfolio, you can grow your wealth over time and secure a brighter future. This subchapter will guide college students on how to start investing and create a diversified portfolio that aligns with their financial goals.

1.   Understanding   the   Basics
Before diving into the world of investing, it's crucial to grasp the fundamentals. Start by learning about different investment vehicles such as stocks, bonds, mutual funds, and real estate. Gain an understanding of risk and return, as well as the importance of diversification.

2.   Determine   Your   Goals
Every investor has unique financial goals. Some seek long-term growth, while others prioritize income generation or capital preservation. Identify your objectives and time horizon to tailor your investment strategy accordingly. Remember, investing is a marathon, not a sprint.

3.   Risk   Tolerance   Assessment
Assessing your risk tolerance is crucial in building an investment portfolio. Determine how comfortable you are with potential fluctuations in the market and adjust your asset allocation accordingly. Generally, younger individuals can take on more risk as they have a longer time horizon to recover from market downturns.

4.   Diversification   is   Key
Diversification is the cornerstone of any successful investment

portfolio. By spreading your investments across different asset classes, industries, and geographical regions, you can mitigate risk and potentially increase returns. Avoid putting all your eggs in one basket.

5.   Start   with   Low-cost   Investments
As college students, it's important to be mindful of fees and expenses. Begin with low-cost investment options such as index funds or exchange-traded funds (ETFs). These passive investment vehicles offer broad market exposure at a fraction of the cost.

6.   Regular   Monitoring   and   Rebalancing
Investing is an ongoing process. Regularly monitor your investments, review their performance, and make adjustments as necessary. Rebalance your portfolio periodically to maintain your desired asset allocation.

7.   Seek   Professional   Guidance
While it's possible to navigate the investment landscape independently, seeking professional guidance can provide valuable insights and expertise. Consider consulting a financial advisor to help you develop a personalized investment plan based on your unique circumstances and goals.

Remember, building an investment portfolio is a long-term commitment. It requires patience, discipline, and continuous learning. By starting early and making informed decisions, college students can lay the foundation for financial success and secure a prosperous future.

Chapter 5: Navigating the Job Market

Resume Writing Tips

Your resume is one of the most important tools you have when it comes to securing a job or internship. It is a snapshot of your skills, qualifications, and experiences, and acts as your first impression to potential employers. In this subchapter, we will explore some valuable resume writing tips that will help you stand out from the competition and increase your chances of landing that dream job.

1. Tailor your resume: Customize your resume for each job application. Read the job description carefully and highlight the skills and experiences that are relevant to the position. This will demonstrate to employers that you are a good fit for the role.

2. Use a professional format: Keep your resume clean, organized, and easy to read. Use a professional font and maintain consistency in formatting. Include clear headings and bullet points to make your resume visually appealing and easy to skim through.

3. Highlight your achievements: Instead of simply listing your responsibilities, focus on your accomplishments. Quantify your achievements wherever possible by using numbers and percentages. This will help employers understand the impact you had in previous roles.

4. Include relevant keywords: Many employers use applicant tracking systems to scan resumes for specific keywords. Research the keywords commonly used in your industry and incorporate them naturally throughout your resume.

5. Keep it concise: Limit your resume to one or two pages, focusing on the most relevant information. Employers typically spend only a few seconds scanning a resume, so make sure your most important qualifications are easily recognizable.

6. Proofread and edit: Always proofread your resume multiple times to ensure there are no spelling or grammatical errors. Ask a friend or mentor to review it as well, as a fresh pair of eyes can often catch mistakes you may have missed.

7. Include a professional summary: Begin your resume with a short summary that highlights your key skills, experiences, and goals. This will grab the attention of employers and provide them with a quick overview of your qualifications.

8. Update your contact information: Double-check that your contact information is accurate and up to date. Include your professional email address and a phone number where you can be easily reached.

Remember, your resume is a marketing tool that represents you and your abilities. By following these resume writing tips, you will be well on your way to creating a compelling resume that will help you achieve success in your career. Take the time to craft a resume that showcases your unique strengths and experiences, and you will greatly increase your chances of landing the job of your dreams.

Job Search Strategies

Subchapter: Job Search Strategies

In today's competitive job market, having a solid plan and implementing effective strategies can make all the difference in securing a fulfilling and financially rewarding career. This subchapter, titled "Job Search Strategies," aims to equip students with practical tips and insights on how to navigate the job search process successfully.

1. Define Your Goals: Before diving into the job search, take the time to reflect on your career aspirations and goals. What industries or roles align with your skills and interests? By clarifying your objectives, you can focus your efforts on opportunities that are the best fit for you.

2. Utilize Career Services: Most colleges and universities offer career services that provide invaluable resources and support. These services often include resume writing assistance, interview preparation, and access to job boards and networking events. Take advantage of these offerings to enhance your chances of finding a job that aligns with your financial and professional goals.

3. Develop Your Personal Brand: In today's digital age, it's important to establish a strong online presence. Create a professional LinkedIn profile and ensure that your social media accounts reflect your desired image to potential employers. Building a personal brand that highlights your skills, experiences, and achievements can significantly boost your visibility and credibility.

4. Network, Network, Network: Networking is a powerful tool in the job search process. Attend industry events, join professional

organizations, and reach out to alumni or professionals in your desired field for informational interviews. Building relationships with individuals who can vouch for your skills and provide insider insights can open doors to hidden job opportunities.

5. Craft an Impressive Resume and Cover Letter: Your resume and cover letter are your first chance to make a positive impression on employers. Tailor your documents to each job application, highlighting relevant skills and experiences. Consider seeking feedback from career counselors or mentors to ensure your application materials stand out from the competition.

6. Prepare for Interviews: Effective interview preparation is essential for demonstrating your suitability for a role. Research the company, practice common interview questions, and develop thoughtful questions to ask the employer. Additionally, consider conducting mock interviews with peers or career advisors to refine your communication skills and boost your confidence.

By implementing these job search strategies, you can increase your chances of finding a fulfilling and financially rewarding career. Remember that perseverance, adaptability, and continuous learning are key to achieving success in the job market. Good luck in your job search endeavors!

Interview Preparation

In today's competitive job market, interview preparation is crucial for students to increase their chances of landing their dream job and achieving financial success. Mastering the art of interviewing requires a combination of self-awareness, research, practice, and effective communication skills. This subchapter will guide you through the essential steps to prepare for an interview and provide you with the tools necessary to impress potential employers.

The first step in interview preparation is self-assessment. Before you can effectively sell yourself, you need to understand your strengths, weaknesses, and career goals. Take the time to identify your skills, experiences, and achievements that make you a valuable candidate. Reflect on your academic accomplishments, extracurricular activities, internships, and any relevant work experience. This self-awareness will help you confidently articulate your value proposition during the interview.

Research is another critical component of interview preparation. Thoroughly investigate the company you are interviewing with. Familiarize yourself with their mission, values, products, services, and recent news. This knowledge will enable you to tailor your responses to align with the organization's goals and demonstrate your genuine interest.

Practice makes perfect, and the same applies to interviews. Prepare responses to common interview questions and practice delivering them confidently and concisely. Consider conducting mock interviews with friends, family members, or career advisors to gain valuable feedback and polish your interviewing skills. Additionally, practice your body language and non-verbal communication to convey professionalism and confidence.

Effective communication skills are vital during an interview. Be prepared to communicate your experiences, skills, and accomplishments in a concise and compelling manner. Develop a list of thoughtful questions to ask the interviewer, demonstrating your interest and engagement. Remember to maintain eye contact, listen actively, and speak clearly and confidently.

Lastly, don't forget about the importance of appearance and punctuality. Dress appropriately for the interview, ensuring that your attire aligns with the company's culture and industry standards. Arrive early to the interview location to allow yourself time to compose and gather your thoughts.

In conclusion, interview preparation is the key to success in today's competitive job market. By following the steps outlined in this subchapter, you will be well-equipped to impress potential employers, showcase your skills, and increase your chances of achieving financial success. Remember to invest time and effort into self-assessment, research, practice, and effective communication skills to master the art of interviewing.

Negotiating Job Offers

Congratulations! After years of hard work, countless interviews, and networking, you have finally received a job offer. It's an exciting time, but before you accept immediately, it's important to remember that negotiations play a crucial role in ensuring your financial success. This subchapter will guide you through the process of negotiating job offers, equipping you with the knowledge and confidence needed to secure your desired compensation package.

1.   Research   and   Preparation: Before entering any negotiation, it is essential to research the industry standards and salary ranges for your position. Use online resources, industry reports, and networking contacts to gather information about average salaries, benefits, and perks. This knowledge will serve as a foundation for your negotiation strategy.

2.   Prioritize   Your   Needs: Identify your financial priorities, such as salary, bonuses, benefits, flexible working hours, or professional development opportunities. Understand what matters most to you, and be prepared to compromise on less critical aspects. This will help you create a clear negotiating strategy.

3.   Art   of   Negotiation: Approach negotiations with confidence and professionalism. Clearly articulate your value, highlighting your achievements, skills, and unique qualities that make you an asset to the company. Be prepared to discuss your research and explain why your desired compensation aligns with industry standards and your qualifications.

4. Consider the Total Compensation Package: Remember that negotiations are not solely about salary. Evaluate the entire compensation package, including health benefits, retirement plans, vacation time, stock options, and opportunities for growth within the company. A comprehensive package can often outweigh a slightly lower salary.

5. Win-Win Solutions: Negotiations should aim for a win-win outcome, where both parties feel satisfied. If the initial offer falls short of your expectations, propose alternative solutions. For example, you could request a performance-based raise after a probationary period, additional vacation days, or educational benefits. Be open to creative options that benefit both you and the employer.

6. Timing is Key: Choose the right moment to negotiate. It is generally advisable to wait until you receive a written offer before initiating negotiations. Express your gratitude for the opportunity and ask for some time to carefully review the offer. This will give you a chance to consider your priorities and formulate a persuasive counteroffer.

Remember, negotiating your job offer is not about being greedy or demanding; it is about advocating for yourself and your financial success. By researching, prioritizing your needs, and approaching negotiations with confidence and professionalism, you can secure a compensation package that reflects your true worth. As a financially literate college student, mastering the art of negotiating job offers is an essential step toward achieving long-term financial success.

Chapter 6: Entrepreneurship and Side Hustles

Exploring Entrepreneurship

In today's rapidly changing world, entrepreneurship has become an increasingly popular and viable career path for many individuals. The concept of turning your passion into a profitable business venture is incredibly enticing, especially for students who are eager to create their own success stories. This subchapter will delve into the exciting world of entrepreneurship, providing valuable insights and guidance for students who aspire to master the art of turning their ideas into lucrative enterprises.

Entrepreneurship is not just about starting a business; it's a mindset that embraces innovation, risk-taking, and the ability to identify and seize opportunities. This subchapter will explore the fundamental principles of entrepreneurship, including the importance of a solid business plan, market research, and understanding your target audience. It will also cover the skills and qualities that successful entrepreneurs possess, such as creativity, resilience, and adaptability.

One crucial aspect of entrepreneurship that will be discussed in this subchapter is the financial aspect. Money is the lifeblood of any business, and understanding how to manage and leverage it effectively is vital for entrepreneurial success. Students will learn about various funding options available to them, such as bootstrapping, angel investors, venture capital, and crowdfunding. They will also gain insights into financial planning, budgeting, and cash flow management, all of which are critical for the sustainability and growth of their ventures.

Furthermore, this subchapter will shed light on the potential challenges and obstacles that entrepreneurs may face, such as competition, market saturation, and economic downturns. Students will learn how to navigate these hurdles and develop strategies for overcoming them, including the importance of continuous learning, networking, and building a strong support system.

To inspire and motivate students, this subchapter will also feature real-life success stories of young entrepreneurs who started from scratch and achieved remarkable financial success. These stories will serve as a testament to the fact that with dedication, perseverance, and the right financial knowledge, anyone can embark on an entrepreneurial journey and achieve their goals.

In conclusion, exploring entrepreneurship is an essential component of mastering money for success. By equipping students with the necessary knowledge, skills, and mindset, this subchapter aims to empower them to confidently pursue their entrepreneurial dreams and create a financially successful future. Whether students aspire to start their own businesses or simply want to develop an entrepreneurial mindset within their chosen careers, this subchapter will provide valuable insights and guidance to help them navigate the exciting world of entrepreneurship.

Identifying Business Opportunities

In today's fast-paced world, the ability to identify and seize promising business opportunities is crucial for achieving financial success. This subchapter will guide you through the process of recognizing potential business ventures and equip you with the essential skills and knowledge needed to navigate the world of entrepreneurship.

1. Developing an entrepreneurial mindset: To identify business opportunities effectively, it is essential to cultivate an entrepreneurial mindset. This involves embracing creativity, risk-taking, and a willingness to think outside the box. By adopting this mindset, you will be better equipped to spot opportunities where others may see obstacles.

2. Identifying market gaps: One of the key aspects of identifying business opportunities is recognizing unmet needs in the market. By conducting thorough market research, you can identify gaps or problems that have yet to be addressed by existing solutions. This could involve observing consumer trends, studying competitors, or conducting surveys and interviews with potential customers.

3. Leveraging your passion and skills: It is often said that success comes from doing what you love. By leveraging your passions and skills, you can identify business opportunities that align with your interests and expertise. This not only increases your chances of success but also ensures that you remain motivated and engaged throughout the entrepreneurial journey.

4. Keeping an eye on emerging trends: The world is constantly evolving, and new trends and technologies present exciting business

opportunities. By staying updated on emerging trends, such as advancements in technology, changes in consumer behavior, or shifts in societal preferences, you can identify potential business ideas that cater to these evolving needs.

5. Network and collaboration: Building a strong network of like-minded individuals and entrepreneurs is crucial for identifying business opportunities. Attend industry events, join relevant organizations, and engage with professionals in your field of interest. Collaborating with others can lead to innovative ideas and joint ventures that may not have been possible otherwise.

6. Evaluating feasibility and viability: Identifying a business opportunity is just the first step. It is essential to evaluate its feasibility and viability. Consider factors such as market demand, competition, financial resources required, and potential profitability. Conduct a thorough analysis to determine if the opportunity aligns with your goals and has the potential for long-term success.

By mastering the art of identifying business opportunities, you are setting yourself up for financial success. Remember, entrepreneurship is not just about identifying an idea; it is about taking action, adapting to challenges, and continuously learning and growing. Embrace the journey, and you will unlock countless possibilities for financial independence and fulfillment.

Developing a Business Plan

In the journey towards financial success, one crucial step is developing a comprehensive business plan. Whether you aspire to start your own business or work for someone else, understanding the process of creating a business plan is essential. This subchapter will guide you through the key elements of a business plan, providing you with a roadmap to success.

A business plan serves as a blueprint for your entrepreneurial endeavors. It outlines your business goals, strategies, and financial projections, helping you stay focused and organized. By developing a well-crafted plan, you demonstrate professionalism, attract potential investors, and increase the likelihood of achieving your financial objectives.

The first section of your business plan should focus on the executive summary. This concise overview provides a snapshot of your entire plan, including your business concept, target market, and competitive advantage. It sets the tone for the rest of the document and should grab the reader's attention.

Next, you should delve into the market analysis. This section requires thorough research to understand your industry, identify your target market, and analyze your competitors. By gathering data and conducting market research, you can determine the demand for your product or service and identify opportunities for growth.

After the market analysis, it's time to outline your business strategy. This includes describing your products or services, pricing strategy, marketing and sales tactics, and operational procedures. A well-defined strategy showcases your understanding of the market and your ability to execute your business plan effectively.

Financial planning is a critical component of any business plan. It involves projecting your revenue, expenses, and cash flow for the next three to five years. By creating realistic financial forecasts and conducting a break-even analysis, you can assess the profitability and sustainability of your business venture.

Lastly, your business plan should include an implementation plan. This section outlines the steps you will take to bring your business to life, including securing funding, acquiring necessary resources, and executing your marketing and sales strategies. It's important to set measurable goals and establish a timeline for achieving them.

Developing a business plan is a vital skill for any aspiring entrepreneur or professional. It requires careful research, strategic thinking, and financial literacy. By mastering the art of business planning, you increase your chances of achieving financial success and turning your entrepreneurial dreams into reality.

Managing Finances as an Entrepreneur

As an aspiring entrepreneur, one of the most crucial skills you need to master is managing your finances effectively. In this subchapter, we will delve into the key aspects of financial management that every entrepreneur should be well-versed in. By understanding how to manage your money wisely, you can lay the foundation for success in your entrepreneurial journey.

1. Budgeting: Creating and sticking to a budget is essential for any entrepreneur. It allows you to track your income and expenses, identify potential areas of overspending, and make informed decisions about resource allocation. Learn how to develop a realistic budget that accounts for both personal and business expenses, and ensure you regularly review and update it as your venture grows.

2. Cash Flow Management: Cash flow is the lifeblood of any business. Understanding how money moves in and out of your business is crucial for making informed decisions. Learn how to forecast your cash flow and manage it effectively, so you can avoid cash shortages and maintain a healthy financial position.

3. Separating Personal and Business Finances: It's vital to keep your personal and business finances separate. This not only simplifies record-keeping but also protects your personal assets in case of any legal issues or financial troubles your business may face. Understand the importance of opening a separate business bank account and maintaining clear financial boundaries.

4. Managing Debt: Debt can be a useful tool for entrepreneurs, but it must be managed responsibly. Learn how to evaluate different types of

debt, such as loans or credit cards, and make informed decisions about when and how to leverage them. Focus on developing a strategy to minimize debt and pay off any outstanding balances efficiently.

5. Tax Planning: Taxes can be complex, but understanding the basics of tax planning will help you navigate this crucial aspect of financial management. Learn about tax deductions, credits, and how to properly document expenses to minimize your tax liability legally. Consider consulting with a tax professional to ensure you are maximizing your tax advantages.

6. Building an Emergency Fund: As an entrepreneur, you must prepare for unexpected financial challenges. Establishing an emergency fund will provide a safety net during tough times. Learn how to set aside a portion of your income regularly and build a reserve that can cover at least three to six months of your living expenses.

By mastering these financial management principles, you will be better equipped to handle the financial complexities of entrepreneurship. Remember, managing your money effectively is not only important for the success of your business but also for your personal financial well-being. With a solid foundation in financial literacy, you will be on the path to achieving your entrepreneurial dreams.

Chapter 7: Insurance and Risk Management

Understanding Insurance Policies

Insurance is an essential component of personal finance and plays a crucial role in ensuring financial security. In this subchapter, we will delve into the intricacies of insurance policies, demystifying complex jargon and providing students with a comprehensive understanding of how insurance works.

Insurance policies are contracts between individuals and insurance companies. They provide protection against financial losses that may arise from unforeseen events or circumstances. There are various types of insurance policies, including health, auto, home, life, and disability insurance, each serving a specific purpose.

One of the fundamental concepts to grasp is the concept of risk. Insurance companies assess risk by considering factors such as age, health, and occupation to determine the premium, which is the amount policyholders pay for coverage. Understanding this concept is crucial as it directly affects the cost and coverage of an insurance policy.

When selecting an insurance policy, it is essential to carefully read and comprehend the terms and conditions. This includes understanding the coverage limits, deductibles, and exclusions. For instance, in an auto insurance policy, the coverage limit determines the maximum amount the insurer will pay in case of an accident. Deductibles refer to the amount the policyholder must pay before the insurance company covers the rest. Exclusions are specific circumstances or events that the insurance policy does not cover. Familiarizing oneself with these aspects will help students make informed decisions when purchasing insurance.

Another critical aspect to consider is the importance of regular review and evaluation of insurance policies. As students progress in their lives and careers, their insurance needs may change. For instance, getting married or starting a family may require additional life insurance coverage. Regularly reviewing insurance policies ensures that students have adequate protection and are not overpaying for unnecessary coverage.

Understanding the claims process is equally important. In the event of a loss or damage covered by the insurance policy, students need to know how to file a claim and the necessary documentation required. Timely and accurate claim submission is vital to ensure a smooth process and receive the necessary compensation.

By comprehending insurance policies, students can make informed decisions about their coverage needs. Insurance is a crucial component of financial planning, providing peace of mind and protection against unexpected events. Mastering this aspect of personal finance is key to building a solid foundation for long-term financial success.

Health Insurance Options

As college students, it is essential to understand the importance of health insurance and the various options available to ensure your well-being. In this subchapter, we will explore different health insurance plans and provide valuable insights into making informed decisions about your coverage. By mastering these options, you will not only protect your health but also ensure financial security in the long run.

1.   Student   Health   Insurance   Plans: Many colleges offer affordable health insurance plans specifically designed for students. These plans often provide comprehensive coverage, including doctor visits, hospitalization, prescription medications, and mental health services. It is crucial to explore the options provided by your college and determine whether they meet your healthcare needs.

2.   Parent's   Health   Insurance: Under the Affordable Care Act, you can stay on your parent's health insurance plan until the age of 26. This can be a cost-effective option, especially if your parents have a comprehensive plan that covers dependents. However, it is important to understand the limitations and ensure that the plan adequately meets your healthcare requirements.

3.   Individual   Health   Insurance   Plans: If you are not eligible for student health insurance or your parent's plan does not suit your needs, you can consider purchasing an individual health insurance plan. These plans are available through state marketplaces or private insurance companies. It is essential to

research and compare the costs and coverage options before selecting a plan.

4. Medicaid and CHIP: Medicaid and the Children's Health Insurance Program (CHIP) provide healthcare coverage for low-income individuals and families. If you meet the eligibility criteria, these programs can be a valuable resource for accessing necessary medical services at little to no cost.

5. Catastrophic Health Insurance: Catastrophic health insurance plans are designed to protect you from major medical expenses in case of a serious illness or injury. These plans typically have lower monthly premiums but higher deductibles. They are an option if you are young, healthy, and primarily seeking coverage for unexpected emergencies.

Understanding the different health insurance options available to you is crucial for your overall well-being and financial success. By carefully evaluating your healthcare needs, comparing plans, and considering your budget, you can make an informed decision that ensures both your health and financial security. Remember, investing in health insurance is an investment in your future, providing peace of mind and protecting you from potential financial burdens.

Renters and Auto Insurance

As college students, many of you may have started living off-campus in rented apartments or houses. Alongside your newfound independence, it's vital to understand the importance of protecting yourself and your belongings through proper insurance coverage. In this subchapter, we will explore the intersection of renters and auto insurance, helping you make informed decisions to safeguard your financial future.

Renters Insurance:

Living in a rented space means you are responsible for your personal belongings and liability. Renters insurance offers coverage against theft, damage, or loss of your personal property due to various covered perils, such as fire, vandalism, or water damage. It also provides liability coverage if someone gets injured in your rented space and decides to sue you for medical expenses or property damage.

When considering renters insurance, evaluate the value of your possessions and the potential risks in your area. It's important to know that your landlord's insurance typically covers only the building structure, not your personal belongings. Renters insurance can help you replace or repair damaged or stolen items, giving you peace of mind.

Auto Insurance:

As students, many of you might own vehicles or rely on cars for commuting to campus. Auto insurance is a legal requirement in most states, and it provides financial protection in case of accidents, theft, or damage to your vehicle. It also covers medical expenses for injuries sustained by you or others involved in the accident. Understanding the different coverage options is essential to make the right choice for your needs.

When selecting auto insurance, consider factors such as liability coverage, collision coverage, comprehensive coverage, and uninsured/underinsured motorist coverage. Liability coverage protects you if you are at fault in an accident and are legally liable for the damages. Collision coverage pays for repairs or replacement of your vehicle if it is damaged in an accident, regardless of fault. Comprehensive coverage covers damage caused by incidents other than collisions, such as theft, vandalism, or natural disasters. Uninsured/underinsured motorist coverage protects you if you are involved in an accident with someone who does not have insurance or insufficient coverage.

Understanding the Relationship:

Renters and auto insurance are often intertwined, particularly when it comes to liability coverage. If a visitor is injured in your rented space or during a car ride, both renters and auto insurance can provide liability coverage. However, it's crucial to review your policies and ensure that you have sufficient coverage in both areas.

By having adequate renters and auto insurance, you protect yourself from potential financial burdens that could arise from unexpected events. Remember to regularly review and update your coverage as your circumstances change, such as acquiring new valuable possessions or moving to a new location.

In conclusion, renting a space and owning a vehicle come with financial responsibilities that can be mitigated through renters and auto insurance. By understanding the importance of these insurance types and making informed choices, you can protect your belongings, yourself, and your financial future.

Protecting Your Financial Future

In today's fast-paced and unpredictable world, it has become more important than ever to take control of your financial future. As college students, you are at a crucial stage in your life where the decisions you make now can have a lasting impact on your financial success. This subchapter will guide you through the essential steps you need to take to protect your financial well-being and ensure a prosperous future.

The first and most crucial step in protecting your financial future is creating a budget. A budget is a roadmap that helps you track your income and expenses, allowing you to make informed decisions about your spending and saving habits. By setting realistic goals and sticking to your budget, you can avoid falling into the trap of unnecessary debt and ensure that you are on the right track towards financial stability.

Another key aspect of protecting your financial future is building an emergency fund. Life is full of unexpected events, such as medical emergencies, car repairs, or sudden job loss. Having a dedicated fund for such emergencies will provide you with a safety net and prevent these unforeseen circumstances from derailing your financial progress.

Insurance is also an essential tool for safeguarding your financial future. Whether it's health insurance, auto insurance, or renter's insurance, having the right coverage can protect you from substantial financial losses in case of accidents or disasters. Understanding the different types of insurance and selecting the appropriate coverage for your needs is critical to ensure your financial security.

Investing in your future is another crucial step towards protecting your financial well-being. While it may seem daunting at first, investing offers the potential for long-term growth and can help you achieve your financial goals. Learning about different investment options, such as stocks, bonds, and mutual funds, will empower you to make informed decisions and take advantage of the power of compounding.

Lastly, staying informed and educated about personal finance is vital to protecting your financial future. Taking the time to read books, attend seminars, or follow reputable financial websites will equip you with the knowledge and skills needed to make smart financial decisions throughout your life.

By following these steps, you will be well on your way to protecting your financial future. Mastering the art of budgeting, building an emergency fund, having the right insurance coverage, investing wisely, and staying informed will set you up for long-term financial success. Remember, the choices you make today will shape your financial future, so start taking control of your financial destiny right now.

Chapter 8: Smart Consumerism

Comparison Shopping

One of the most valuable skills you can develop as a college student is comparison shopping. Whether it's buying textbooks, groceries, or even a new laptop, being able to compare prices and make informed choices can save you a significant amount of money in the long run. In this subchapter, we will explore the importance of comparison shopping and provide you with some useful tips to become a savvy consumer.

Why is comparison shopping important? Well, let's face it, as students, we often have limited funds, and every dollar counts. By comparing prices and quality, you can stretch your budget further and ensure you are getting the best bang for your buck. Comparison shopping also helps you become a discerning consumer, enabling you to make more confident and informed purchasing decisions.

When it comes to comparison shopping, there are a few key steps to follow. First, identify what you need and set a budget. Knowing exactly what you're looking for and how much you can afford will help narrow down your options. Next, research different retailers or online platforms that offer the product you're interested in. Check out their prices, read reviews, and compare the features or specifications. Don't forget to consider factors like warranty, customer service, and return policies as well.

To make your comparison shopping even more effective, utilize online tools and resources. Many websites and apps offer price comparison features that allow you to see the prices from different sellers all in one place. Additionally, consider joining student discount programs or using coupon codes to further reduce costs. Remember, a few extra minutes spent on comparing prices can lead to significant savings.

It's important to note that comparison shopping is not limited to physical products. You can also apply this technique when choosing services like insurance, phone plans, or even housing options. By comparing rates and terms, you can find the best deals and avoid potential financial pitfalls.

In conclusion, comparison shopping is an essential skill for college students aiming to master their money. By taking the time to research, compare prices, and consider various factors, you can make wise financial decisions that will benefit you in the long run. So, before making any purchase, big or small, remember to comparison shop. Your wallet will thank you!

Understanding Consumer Rights

As college students, it is crucial to have a strong understanding of consumer rights to effectively navigate the world of personal finance. In this subchapter, we will delve into the importance of consumer rights and how they can contribute to your financial success.

Consumer rights refer to the set of laws and protections in place to ensure fair and ethical treatment for individuals engaging in business transactions. These rights empower consumers by safeguarding their interests, promoting transparency, and providing avenues for redress in case of any grievances. By understanding and exercising your consumer rights, you can make informed financial decisions and protect yourself from fraudulent practices.

One fundamental consumer right is the right to information. It is essential to obtain complete and accurate information about a product or service before making a purchase. This includes understanding the terms and conditions, warranties, return policies, and any associated costs. By doing so, you can make well-informed choices that align with your financial goals.

Another significant consumer right is the right to safety. This encompasses the assurance that the products and services you purchase are safe and reliable. It is crucial to be aware of product recalls and stay informed about potential risks associated with certain items. By exercising this right, you can protect your health, well-being, and financial investment.

Consumer rights also encompass the right to privacy and the protection of personal information. In an increasingly digital world, it is crucial to be aware of your data privacy rights and the steps you can take to safeguard your personal information. By understanding how your data is collected, used, and shared, you can make informed decisions about sharing your personal information and protect yourself from potential identity theft or fraud.

In case of any issues or disputes, it is important to be aware of your right to redress. This includes the right to seek compensation, refunds, or repairs for faulty products or unsatisfactory services. By understanding the avenues available to you, such as contacting consumer protection agencies or seeking legal advice, you can seek appropriate remedies and protect your financial interests.

In conclusion, understanding consumer rights is essential for college students on their journey towards financial success. By being aware of your rights, you can make informed decisions, protect yourself from fraudulent practices, and seek redress when necessary. Empower yourself with knowledge and take charge of your financial well-being through a comprehensive understanding of consumer rights.

Avoiding Identity Theft

Subchapter: Avoiding Identity Theft

In today's digital age, where financial transactions are increasingly conducted online, the risk of identity theft has become a significant concern. As college students, it is crucial to be aware of the dangers and take necessary precautions to protect your financial information. This subchapter aims to equip you with the knowledge and strategies to avoid falling victim to identity theft and its devastating consequences.

1.   Understanding   Identity   Theft: Identity theft occurs when someone steals your personal information, such as your Social Security number, bank account details, or credit card information, to commit fraud or other criminal activities. It can result in severe financial loss, damage to your credit score, and even legal troubles.

2.   Strong   Passwords: One of the simplest yet most effective ways to safeguard your online accounts is by using strong, unique passwords. Avoid using easily guessable information like your birthdate or pet's name. Instead, opt for a combination of uppercase and lowercase letters, numbers, and special characters. Additionally, consider using a password manager to secure and manage all your passwords.

3.   Be   Wary   of   Phishing: Phishing is a common tactic used by hackers to trick individuals into revealing their sensitive information. Be cautious of emails, text messages, or calls that request personal or financial details. Legitimate

institutions would never ask for this information via email or phone. When in doubt, contact the company directly through their official website or customer service hotline.

4. Secure Your Devices: Protecting your electronic devices is essential in preventing identity theft. Ensure that your smartphone, laptop, and other gadgets have up-to-date antivirus software and firewalls installed. Set up a strong PIN or password to access your devices, and enable biometric authentication methods like fingerprint or facial recognition for an added layer of security.

5. Monitor Your Accounts: Regularly monitoring your bank accounts, credit cards, and other financial accounts can help you detect any unauthorized activity promptly. Set up transaction alerts and review your statements carefully. If you notice any suspicious transactions or discrepancies, notify your financial institution immediately.

6. Safeguard Your Social Security Number: Your Social Security number (SSN) is a prime target for identity thieves. Only provide it when absolutely necessary and avoid carrying your Social Security card with you. Store any physical documents containing your SSN in a secure location, such as a locked drawer or safe.

By implementing these proactive measures, you can significantly reduce the risk of falling victim to identity theft. Remember, your financial well-being is crucial for your success as a college student. Stay vigilant, protect your personal information, and enjoy peace of mind knowing that you are taking the necessary steps to secure your financial future.

Making Informed Financial Decisions

In today's fast-paced world, financial literacy is crucial for success, especially for college students. Understanding how to make informed financial decisions is a skill that will serve you well throughout your life. This subchapter aims to provide you with the necessary knowledge and tools to navigate the often confusing world of personal finance.

One of the first steps to making informed financial decisions is understanding your current financial situation. This includes knowing your income, expenses, and debt. By creating a budget, you can track your spending habits and identify areas where you can cut back to save money. This will help you develop a realistic plan for achieving your financial goals.

Another key aspect of making informed financial decisions is knowing how to evaluate financial products and services. Whether it's choosing a bank account, credit card, or investment option, it's important to compare different options and read the fine print. Understanding the fees, interest rates, and terms and conditions will ensure that you make the best choice for your financial needs.

Additionally, learning about the different types of investments and the concept of risk versus reward is essential for building wealth. From stocks and bonds to real estate and mutual funds, there are various ways to grow your money over time. However, it's important to understand the potential risks involved and to diversify your investments to mitigate those risks.

Being informed also means understanding how to protect yourself from scams and fraud. As a college student, you may be targeted by scammers looking to take advantage of your lack of financial experience. By learning to identify red flags, protecting your personal information, and being cautious with online transactions, you can minimize the risk of falling victim to financial scams.

Lastly, seeking out financial education resources and professional advice can greatly enhance your financial literacy. There are numerous books, websites, and workshops available that can provide valuable insights into managing money effectively. Additionally, consulting with a financial advisor can help you make more informed decisions tailored to your specific financial situation and goals.

In conclusion, mastering the art of making informed financial decisions is essential for college students seeking success. By understanding your financial situation, evaluating financial products, investing wisely, protecting yourself from scams, and seeking out knowledge, you can take control of your finances and pave the way to a financially secure future. Remember, financial literacy is a lifelong journey, and the skills you develop now will benefit you for years to come.

Chapter 9: Financial Independence and Future Planning

Building an Emergency Fund

One of the most important steps towards financial success is building an emergency fund. As college students, we often find ourselves facing unexpected expenses or financial emergencies. Whether it's a medical bill, a car repair, or a sudden job loss, having a safety net in the form of an emergency fund can provide peace of mind and help us navigate through these challenging times.

So, what exactly is an emergency fund? It is a dedicated savings account that is specifically set aside for unexpected expenses. The purpose of this fund is to cover unforeseen financial emergencies without having to rely on credit cards or loans. By having an emergency fund, you can avoid going into debt and maintain financial stability.

But how do you build an emergency fund? The first step is to establish a savings goal. It's recommended to aim for at least three to six months' worth of living expenses. This may seem like a daunting task, especially for students, but start small and work your way up. Even saving a little each month can make a difference.

To begin, create a budget to track your income and expenses. Look for areas where you can cut back or save money, such as reducing dining out expenses or finding cheaper alternatives for entertainment. Every time you receive income, allocate a portion towards your emergency fund.

Consider automating your savings by setting up an automatic transfer from your checking account to your emergency fund. This way, you won't have to worry about forgetting to save or being tempted to spend the money elsewhere. Treat your emergency fund contribution as a monthly bill that must be paid.

Additionally, consider earning extra income through part-time jobs or gig work. By dedicating this additional income solely to your emergency fund, you can accelerate your savings and reach your goal faster.

Remember, building an emergency fund requires discipline and commitment. It may take time, but the financial security and peace of mind it provides are priceless. Start today, no matter how small the contribution, and watch your emergency fund grow over time. You never know when you might need it, but when an unexpected expense arises, you'll be grateful that you took the time to build your safety net.

In conclusion, building an emergency fund is an essential step towards financial success. By setting a savings goal, creating a budget, automating savings, and seeking additional income opportunities, college students can establish a safety net that will protect them from unexpected financial emergencies. Start building your emergency fund today and gain the peace of mind that comes with financial stability.

Retirement Planning for Students

Introduction:
As a student, retirement planning might be the last thing on your mind. With exams, assignments, and a busy social life, it's easy to overlook the importance of planning for your future. However, starting to save for retirement at an early age can make a significant difference in your financial well-being later in life. In this subchapter, we will explore the concept of retirement planning specifically tailored to students, offering valuable insights and advice to help you secure a financially successful future.

The Power of Compound Interest:
One of the key advantages students have when it comes to retirement planning is time. The power of compound interest cannot be underestimated. By starting early, even with small amounts, your money can grow exponentially over time. We will delve into the concept of compound interest and demonstrate how starting to save for retirement now can greatly benefit you in the long run.

Budgeting and Saving:
Budgeting and saving go hand in hand when it comes to retirement planning. We will provide practical tips and strategies for creating a budget that allows you to save a portion of your income for retirement. From tracking expenses to cutting unnecessary costs, we will help you develop the habits necessary to build a strong financial foundation for your future.

Investment Options for Students:
While saving money is crucial, investing wisely can further accelerate

your retirement savings. We will introduce you to various investment options suitable for students, such as individual retirement accounts (IRAs), index funds, and low-cost exchange-traded funds (ETFs). Additionally, we will discuss the importance of diversifying your investments and the potential risks associated with different investment choices.

Planning for Life After College:
As you prepare to enter the workforce after college, it's crucial to understand the retirement benefits offered by your employer. We will guide you through the process of evaluating job offers and weighing the retirement benefits they provide. Additionally, we will emphasize the significance of contributing to employer-sponsored retirement plans, such as 401(k)s, and the advantages they offer.

Conclusion:
Retirement planning may seem like a distant concern for students, but the earlier you start, the better off you'll be in the long run. By taking advantage of compound interest, budgeting, saving, and making smart investment choices, you can set yourself up for financial success in retirement. This subchapter aims to equip you with the knowledge and tools necessary to begin your retirement planning journey. Remember, it's never too early to start securing your future.

Estate Planning Basics

As a college student, you may think that estate planning is something that only older adults need to worry about. However, understanding the basics of estate planning is crucial for everyone, regardless of age or financial status. Estate planning is not just about distributing your assets after death; it is a comprehensive strategy that ensures your financial well-being and protects your loved ones in case of unexpected events.

One of the primary goals of estate planning is to create a plan for the distribution of your assets. This includes everything you own, such as money, property, investments, and even digital assets like social media accounts and cryptocurrencies. By creating a will or trust, you can determine how your assets will be distributed, ensuring that your wishes are respected and your loved ones are taken care of.

Estate planning also involves making important decisions regarding healthcare and end-of-life wishes. By creating advance healthcare directives, such as a living will or healthcare power of attorney, you can ensure that your medical preferences are known and followed in case you become unable to communicate them yourself. This not only provides peace of mind for you but also relieves your loved ones from the burden of making difficult medical decisions on your behalf.

Another critical aspect of estate planning is minimizing taxes and expenses. By employing various strategies, such as gifting, establishing trusts, or setting up life insurance policies, you can potentially reduce the tax burden on your estate and maximize the amount of wealth passed on to your beneficiaries.

While estate planning may seem daunting, especially for college students, it is never too early to start. By starting early, you can take advantage of the power of compounding and make informed financial decisions that align with your long-term goals. It is important to remember that estate planning is an ongoing process that should be reviewed and updated regularly to reflect changes in your financial situation, family dynamics, and personal goals.

In conclusion, estate planning basics are essential for students looking to achieve financial success. By understanding the importance of creating a comprehensive estate plan, you can protect your assets, ensure your wishes are met, and provide financial security for your loved ones. Take the time to educate yourself about estate planning, consult with professionals if necessary, and be proactive in taking control of your financial future. Remember, mastering money is not just about accumulating wealth, but also about securing it for your own success and the success of future generations.

Long-Term Financial Goals

In today's fast-paced world, it is crucial for college students to develop a solid understanding of financial literacy. Mastering the art of money management is not only important for surviving the college years, but it also sets the foundation for long-term success. This subchapter, "Long-Term Financial Goals," aims to guide students towards establishing financial objectives that will pave the way for a prosperous future.

Setting long-term financial goals is essential as it provides a sense of direction and enables students to make informed decisions about their money. By defining clear objectives, students can prioritize their spending, saving, and investing habits. Whether it's starting a business, buying a house, or retiring early, these goals provide a roadmap to achieve financial independence.

One crucial aspect of long-term financial planning is understanding the power of compound interest. By starting to invest early, even with small amounts, students can harness the magic of compounding and watch their savings grow exponentially over time. This subchapter will delve into the importance of starting to save early and the concept of compound interest, offering strategies to maximize its benefits.

Additionally, it is vital for students to learn about the various investment options available to them. From stocks and bonds to mutual funds and real estate, understanding the pros and cons of each investment vehicle is crucial for making informed decisions. Exploring different investment strategies and risk management techniques will empower students to build a diversified portfolio that aligns with their long-term financial goals.

Furthermore, this subchapter will emphasize the significance of creating an emergency fund. Life is filled with unexpected events and having a safety net in place is essential for financial stability. Students will learn how to allocate a portion of their income towards an emergency fund, ensuring they are prepared to handle any unforeseen circumstances without derailing their long-term financial objectives.

In conclusion, "Long-Term Financial Goals" is a subchapter designed to equip students with the necessary knowledge and skills to establish a strong financial foundation. By understanding the power of compound interest, exploring different investment options, and creating an emergency fund, students can set themselves up for a lifetime of financial success. Remember, the decisions you make today regarding your money can significantly impact your future, so start planning for your financial goals now and reap the benefits in the long run.

Chapter 10: Building Wealth and Giving Back

Investing in Stocks and Bonds

Welcome to the subchapter on investing in stocks and bonds, an essential component of financial literacy that will set you on the path to money and success. Understanding the world of investing is crucial for college students as it provides an opportunity to grow your wealth over time and achieve financial goals.

Stocks and bonds are two primary investment options that offer distinct advantages and risks. Let's explore each of them in detail.

Stocks, also known as shares or equities, represent ownership in a company. Investing in stocks allows you to become a part-owner and benefit from the company's growth and profitability. As a shareholder, you have the potential to earn returns through dividends (a portion of the company's profits distributed to shareholders) and capital appreciation (increase in the stock's value over time). However, stocks also carry risks, as their value can fluctuate due to various factors such as economic conditions, company performance, or market sentiment.

Bonds, on the other hand, are debt securities issued by governments, municipalities, or corporations. When you invest in bonds, you essentially lend money to the issuer for a specific period, in return for regular interest payments and the repayment of the principal amount at maturity. Bonds are generally considered less risky than stocks, as they provide a fixed income stream and are less affected by market volatility. However, it's important to assess the creditworthiness of the issuer and understand the potential risks associated with interest rate changes.

Before diving into the world of stocks and bonds, it's crucial to develop an investment strategy. This includes setting clear financial goals, understanding your risk tolerance, and diversifying your portfolio. Diversification involves spreading your investments across different asset classes and industries to minimize risk. Additionally, staying informed about the market trends, conducting thorough research, and seeking advice from financial professionals will enhance your investment decision-making process.

Investing in stocks and bonds requires a long-term perspective and patience. It's essential to remember that the value of your investments can fluctuate, and short-term market movements should not deter you from your long-term goals. Regularly reviewing and rebalancing your portfolio is crucial to ensure it aligns with your changing financial needs and goals.

In conclusion, investing in stocks and bonds offers college students an opportunity for financial success. By understanding the basics, developing a strategy, and staying informed, you can navigate the investment landscape and make informed decisions. Remember, investing is a journey, and with time, knowledge, and discipline, you can maximize your financial potential and achieve your long-term goals.

Real Estate Investment Opportunities

Real estate has always been considered a lucrative investment opportunity, and with good reason. The potential for generating substantial wealth through real estate investments is unparalleled. In this subchapter, we will explore the various real estate investment opportunities available to students and how they can harness the power of real estate to secure their financial success.

1. Rental Properties: One of the most common real estate investment opportunities is buying rental properties. As a student, you can consider investing in a property near your college or university. Renting out rooms or apartments to fellow students can provide a steady stream of income that can help cover your mortgage payments while also building equity in the property.

2. Real Estate Investment Trusts (REITs): For students looking for a more passive investment approach, REITs offer an excellent opportunity. REITs are companies that own, operate, or finance income-generating real estate. By investing in REITs, you can become a shareholder and benefit from the rental income and appreciation of the properties they own.

3. House Flipping: If you have an eye for design and a knack for renovation, house flipping can be a profitable venture. The idea is to purchase a distressed property, renovate it, and sell it for a higher price. While it requires careful planning and management, successful house flipping can yield substantial profits.

4. Real Estate Crowdfunding: Another emerging opportunity for students is real estate crowdfunding. This involves pooling money

with other investors to fund real estate projects. Through online platforms, you can invest in various projects such as commercial properties, residential developments, or even vacation rentals. Real estate crowdfunding allows students to invest with smaller amounts and diversify their investments across multiple properties.

5. Real Estate Investment Clubs: Joining a real estate investment club can provide students with valuable networking opportunities and access to experienced investors. These clubs often organize seminars, workshops, and property tours to help members learn and explore potential investment opportunities. Being part of such a club can provide insights, mentorship, and even potential partnerships for your real estate investments.

Remember, real estate investment opportunities require careful evaluation, planning, and research. It is essential to understand the local real estate market, analyze the potential risks and returns, and have a long-term investment strategy. Real estate investments can be highly rewarding, but they also require commitment, patience, and a willingness to learn from both successes and failures.

By exploring these various real estate investment opportunities, students can start their journey toward financial success, building wealth, and securing their financial future.

Philanthropy and Giving Back

In our journey towards financial success, it is essential to understand the significance of philanthropy and giving back. While the pursuit of wealth may be a personal goal, true success lies in utilizing our resources to make a positive impact on the world around us. This chapter will delve into the importance of philanthropy, how it can enhance our lives, and ways to incorporate giving back into our financial plans.

Philanthropy, at its core, is the act of using our time, talents, and financial resources to support charitable causes. It allows us to contribute to the betterment of society and make a difference in the lives of others. While many students may assume that philanthropy is reserved for the wealthy, it is crucial to recognize that even small acts of giving can create a ripple effect of change.

Engaging in philanthropy offers numerous benefits beyond the positive impact it has on the community. By giving back, we develop a sense of gratitude for our own blessings and gain a deeper understanding of the challenges faced by others. Furthermore, philanthropy provides opportunities for personal growth, networking, and skill development. Volunteering or supporting charitable organizations can help us build valuable connections, enhance our leadership abilities, and broaden our perspectives.

Integrating philanthropy into our financial plans is not only a moral responsibility but also a smart financial move. By setting aside a portion of our income for charitable contributions, we cultivate a mindset of abundance and generosity. Moreover, contributing to nonprofits and causes aligned with our values can provide tax benefits and reduce our taxable income.

To incorporate giving back into our financial plan, we must begin by identifying the causes we are passionate about. Whether it's education, environmental preservation, or healthcare, finding a cause that resonates with us will make our philanthropic efforts more fulfilling. We can then research and support organizations that align with our chosen cause, either through donations or volunteering our time and skills.

Lastly, it is crucial to approach philanthropy with intention and thoughtfulness. Rather than engaging in random acts of giving, we should strive for strategic philanthropy. This involves conducting due diligence on the organizations we support, evaluating their impact, and ensuring that our contributions are being utilized effectively.

In conclusion, philanthropy and giving back are integral components of achieving financial success. By incorporating giving into our financial plans, we not only make a positive impact on society but also enhance our personal growth and sense of purpose. So, let us embrace the power of philanthropy and use our resources to create a more compassionate and prosperous world for all.

Achieving Financial Freedom

In this subchapter, we will explore the concept of achieving financial freedom and provide you with essential tips and strategies to help you on your journey towards financial independence. As students, it is crucial to develop a strong foundation in managing your finances to set yourself up for long-term success.

Financial freedom refers to the state of having enough money to cover your expenses and pursue your goals without being reliant on others. It is about taking control of your financial situation and making informed decisions to create a secure and prosperous future.

To achieve financial freedom, the first step is to establish a budget. Create a comprehensive plan that outlines your income, expenses, and savings goals. Stick to this budget and regularly review it to ensure you are on track. By understanding where your money goes, you can make conscious choices and prioritize your spending.

Another crucial aspect of achieving financial freedom is managing debt effectively. College students often face student loans and credit card debt. Develop a strategy to pay off your debt systematically, starting with high-interest debt first. Consider consolidating or refinancing your loans to reduce interest rates. By taking control of your debt, you can free up more money for savings and investment.

Saving and investing are essential components of achieving financial freedom. Start by building an emergency fund to cover unexpected expenses. Aim to save at least three to six months' worth of living expenses. Once you have an emergency fund, focus on long-term investments, such as retirement accounts or stock market investments.

The power of compounding can work in your favor over time, allowing your money to grow exponentially.

Additionally, mastering the art of investing wisely is vital. Educate yourself about different investment options and seek professional advice if needed. Diversify your investments to spread the risk and maximize potential returns.

Finally, it is crucial to develop good financial habits. Practice delayed gratification and avoid impulsive spending. Set realistic financial goals and work towards them diligently. Surround yourself with like-minded individuals who prioritize financial literacy and success. Continuous learning and self-improvement in the realm of personal finance will empower you to make informed decisions that align with your long-term goals.

In summary, achieving financial freedom is a journey that requires discipline, patience, and commitment. By creating a budget, managing debt, saving, investing, and developing good financial habits, you can pave the way for a secure financial future. Start early, stay consistent, and remember that financial freedom is within your reach.

Chapter 11: Financial Resources for College Students

Scholarships and Grants

Scholarships and Grants: Unlocking Financial Success for College Students

In the journey towards financial success, college students often face numerous challenges. From tuition fees and textbooks to housing and living expenses, the financial burden can seem overwhelming. However, there is good news: scholarships and grants offer a lifeline for students seeking to alleviate this burden and pave the way to a brighter future. In this subchapter, we will explore the world of scholarships and grants, empowering you with the knowledge to secure these valuable resources.

Scholarships are merit-based awards that recognize and reward exceptional academic achievements, talents, or specific skills. They are often offered by schools, private organizations, or corporations. The key to accessing scholarships is to thoroughly research and identify the ones that align with your academic pursuits, extracurricular activities, or personal background. By tailoring your applications to match the scholarship criteria, you enhance your chances of success.

Grants, on the other hand, are primarily need-based and provide financial assistance to students facing financial hardships. These grants can come from federal, state, or institutional sources. Filling out the Free Application for Federal Student Aid (FAFSA) is the first step in determining your eligibility for various grants. By providing accurate information about your family's financial situation, you can unlock potential grant opportunities to lighten your financial load.

It is essential to approach scholarships and grants proactively. Start your search early, as many deadlines occur months before the academic year begins. Utilize online scholarship databases, financial aid offices, and community organizations to discover lesser-known opportunities. Remember that persistence and determination can pay off, so don't give up easily.

Additionally, cultivating a strong application is crucial. Create a compelling personal statement that highlights your unique attributes, experiences, and goals. Ensure your academic records are exemplary, and solicit recommendation letters from mentors, teachers, or employers who can vouch for your abilities and character.

Lastly, be aware of any scholarship or grant requirements that may demand ongoing academic performance or community involvement. Maintaining high grades and actively participating in extracurricular activities can help secure the continuation of financial support throughout your college journey.

Scholarships and grants hold immense potential for college students, providing not only financial relief but also recognition for your hard work and dedication. Mastering the art of scholarship applications and grant eligibility is a vital step towards financial literacy and securing a brighter future. So, take charge of your financial success, explore the vast array of scholarships and grants available, and unlock the doors to a world of opportunities!

Financial Aid Programs

In today's economic landscape, pursuing higher education can come with a hefty price tag. The rising costs of tuition, textbooks, and living expenses can be daunting for students and their families. However, there is good news – financial aid programs exist to help alleviate some of the financial burden and make college more accessible to all.

Financial aid programs are designed to provide students with the necessary funds to pursue their educational goals. These programs can come in the form of scholarships, grants, work-study opportunities, or loans. Understanding the different types of financial aid programs and how to navigate them is crucial for students seeking financial support.

Scholarships are a popular form of financial aid that do not require repayment. They are typically based on academic merit, athletic abilities, artistic talents, or other criteria. Scholarships can be awarded by colleges, private organizations, or government entities. It is important for students to research and apply for scholarships that align with their interests and achievements to maximize their chances of receiving financial aid.

Grants are another form of financial aid that do not require repayment. Unlike scholarships, grants are usually need-based and can be provided by the federal government, state governments, or colleges themselves. Students must fill out the Free Application for Federal Student Aid (FAFSA) to determine their eligibility for grants. Applying for grants early is essential as funds are limited and awarded on a first-come, first-served basis.

Work-study programs offer students the opportunity to work part-time while attending college. These programs provide students with valuable work experience and a means to contribute towards their educational expenses. Work-study jobs are typically located on campus and offer flexible schedules to accommodate students' class schedules.

Loans are another option for students who require financial assistance. Unlike scholarships, grants, or work-study programs, loans must be repaid with interest. There are different types of loans available, including federal student loans and private loans. It is important for students to understand the terms and conditions of loans, including interest rates and repayment plans, before committing to them.

In conclusion, financial aid programs are invaluable resources for students seeking financial assistance to pursue higher education. Scholarships, grants, work-study programs, and loans all play a significant role in making college more affordable. It is crucial for students to research and apply for these programs early, as competition can be fierce. By understanding the different types of financial aid programs available and how to navigate them, students can set themselves up for success in their academic journey without being burdened by excessive debt.

Campus Resources for Financial Assistance

As a college student, managing your finances can be a challenging task. From tuition fees to living expenses, it's no secret that the cost of education can be overwhelming. However, there are numerous campus resources available to help you navigate the world of financial assistance and ensure your success.

One of the first places to start is the financial aid office on campus. This department is dedicated to helping students secure the necessary funds to pay for their education. They can guide you through the process of applying for scholarships, grants, and loans. Additionally, they can provide valuable information on work-study opportunities, which allow you to earn money while gaining valuable experience.

Scholarships are a popular form of financial assistance that can greatly alleviate the burden of tuition costs. Many colleges offer scholarships based on academic merit, extracurricular activities, or specific fields of study. The financial aid office can help you identify and apply for these scholarships, increasing your chances of receiving financial support.

Grants are another option worth exploring. Unlike loans, grants do not have to be repaid, making them an attractive form of financial assistance. They are typically awarded based on financial need, and the financial aid office can assist you in determining your eligibility and applying for grants.

Another valuable resource on campus is the career services office. While their primary focus may be on helping students find employment after graduation, they can also provide guidance on internships and part-time jobs during your college years. Working part-time not only provides you with a steady income but also teaches valuable skills that can enhance your resume.

Some colleges also have emergency funds available for students facing unexpected financial hardships. These funds can be a lifeline during difficult times, such as medical emergencies or unexpected expenses. Reach out to the financial aid office to inquire about these resources and learn about the application process.

In conclusion, mastering your money is crucial for success as a college student. By utilizing the campus resources available to you, such as the financial aid office, scholarships, grants, work-study opportunities, and emergency funds, you can alleviate the financial burden and focus on your studies. Take advantage of these resources to ensure a successful and financially secure college experience.

Online Tools and Apps for Money Management

In today's digital age, managing your money has become easier than ever before. With the advent of online tools and apps, students now have the power to take control of their finances and pave the way for a successful future. In this subchapter, we will explore some of the best online tools and apps available for money management, specifically tailored to the needs of students.

1. Mint: Mint is a popular and comprehensive personal finance app that allows you to track your spending, create budgets, and set financial goals. It also provides insights into your financial habits and offers suggestions for saving money.

2. Acorns: Acorns is an investment app that automatically invests your spare change by rounding up your purchases and investing the difference. It's a great way to start building wealth while studying, as Acorns intelligently invests your money in diversified portfolios.

3. Venmo: Venmo is a peer-to-peer payment app that allows you to send and receive money from friends and family instantly. It's perfect for splitting bills, paying rent, or reimbursing friends for shared expenses.

4. You Need a Budget (YNAB): YNAB is an online tool that helps you allocate your income to different categories, such as rent, groceries, and entertainment. It encourages you to live within your means and save for future expenses.

5. Splitwise: Splitwise is a handy app for tracking shared expenses, especially for students living with roommates. It simplifies splitting

bills and helps avoid money-related conflicts by keeping everyone accountable.

6. PocketGuard: PocketGuard is a personal finance app that gives you an overview of your financial situation in real-time. It tracks your income, bills, and spending to help you stay on top of your finances and avoid overspending.

7. Goodbudget: Goodbudget is a budgeting app that uses the envelope budgeting method. It helps you allocate money for different categories and tracks your spending to ensure you don't exceed your budget.

By leveraging these online tools and apps, students can take control of their finances and set themselves up for future success. Whether it's tracking expenses, creating budgets, or investing spare change, these tools offer convenience, efficiency, and peace of mind. Remember, mastering money management is a crucial skill that will serve you well throughout your college years and beyond. So, download these apps, embrace the power of technology, and embark on your journey towards financial literacy and success.

Chapter 12: Maintaining Financial Wellness

Setting Realistic Financial Expectations

When it comes to managing your money, setting realistic financial expectations is crucial to achieving financial success. As college students, you are at a pivotal stage in your life where financial decisions can have a long-lasting impact on your future. Understanding how to set realistic financial expectations will empower you to make informed choices and pave the way for a secure financial future.

First and foremost, it is essential to acknowledge that financial success does not happen overnight. It requires consistent effort, discipline, and patience. Many students often fall into the trap of expecting quick financial gains or succumbing to the allure of get-rich-quick schemes. However, building wealth is a gradual process that requires careful planning and wise money management.

One key aspect of setting realistic financial expectations is understanding your current financial situation. Take stock of your income, expenses, and debts. Assess your financial goals and determine what steps you need to take to achieve them. It is crucial to be honest with yourself and set achievable milestones along the way. This may include creating a budget, saving a certain percentage of your income, or paying off high-interest debts.

Moreover, it is important to be mindful of the difference between needs and wants. While it is natural to desire certain luxuries or indulgences, it is crucial to prioritize your financial well-being. Setting realistic expectations means distinguishing between what is necessary for your daily life and what is merely a desire. By focusing on your needs and avoiding unnecessary expenses, you can better allocate your resources toward achieving your financial goals.

Another essential aspect of setting realistic financial expectations is understanding that setbacks and unexpected expenses are a part of life. Emergencies, medical bills, or unforeseen circumstances can disrupt even the most carefully planned financial journey. It is vital to have a contingency plan in place and maintain an emergency fund to cushion yourself during such times. By expecting the unexpected and being prepared, you can minimize the impact of financial setbacks on your overall financial health.

In conclusion, setting realistic financial expectations is crucial for college students to achieve financial success. It requires understanding your current financial situation, distinguishing between needs and wants, and being prepared for unexpected expenses. By adopting a patient and disciplined approach to money management, you can pave the way for a secure financial future. Remember, building wealth is a gradual process, and with the right mindset and actions, you can attain financial stability and success.

Overcoming Financial Challenges

Introduction:

In today's competitive world, achieving success often requires more than just academic excellence. It demands a solid understanding of money management and the ability to overcome financial challenges. This subchapter aims to equip college students with the necessary knowledge and skills to navigate financial obstacles and pave the way for a successful future.

1.   Budgeting:

The first step towards overcoming financial challenges is creating a budget. By understanding your income and expenses, you can prioritize your spending and identify areas where you can cut back. This will not only help you live within your means but also allow you to allocate funds towards achieving your long-term goals.

2.   Minimizing   Debt:

Student loans, credit card debt, and other liabilities can hinder your financial progress. This section will provide strategies for minimizing debt, such as paying more than the minimum balance, negotiating interest rates, and exploring loan forgiveness programs. By taking control of your debt, you can alleviate financial stress and set yourself up for success.

3.   Saving   and   Investing:

Building a strong financial foundation involves saving and investing wisely. This subchapter will explain the importance of an emergency fund and guide you on how to save a portion of your income regularly.

Additionally, it will introduce the basics of investing, such as stocks, bonds, and mutual funds, to help you grow your wealth over time.

4.   Part-Time   Jobs   and   Internships: Finding part-time jobs and internships not only provides you with additional income but also valuable work experience. This section will explore different employment opportunities, highlight the benefits of internships, and provide tips on how to balance work and academics successfully.

5.   Financial   Aid   and   Scholarships: Many students face financial challenges due to the high cost of education. This subchapter will delve into available financial aid options, including scholarships, grants, and work-study programs. It will also provide guidance on how to search for scholarships and maximize your chances of securing them.

6.   Entrepreneurship   and   Side   Hustles: In today's gig economy, entrepreneurship and side hustles can be lucrative avenues for generating income. This section will inspire students to explore their entrepreneurial spirit, sharing stories of successful student entrepreneurs and providing practical steps to start a side business while in college.

Conclusion:
Overcoming financial challenges is a crucial aspect of achieving success. By implementing the strategies and techniques outlined in this subchapter, students can gain financial literacy and develop the skills required to navigate the complexities of money management. With a strong financial foundation, they will be better equipped to

pursue their dreams, secure their future, and ultimately thrive in the world of money for success.

Seeking Professional Financial Advice

When it comes to managing our finances, it's easy to feel overwhelmed and unsure of where to begin. Many students are entering college with little to no experience in handling money, which can lead to financial difficulties and stress down the road. That's where seeking professional financial advice becomes crucial.

Professional financial advice is essential for students who want to achieve financial success. It provides valuable insights and guidance tailored to individual circumstances, helping students make informed decisions about their money. Here are a few reasons why seeking professional financial advice is so important:

1. Knowledge and Expertise: Financial advisors have extensive knowledge and expertise in various aspects of personal finance. They understand the complexities of budgeting, saving, investing, and debt management. By seeking their advice, students can tap into this wealth of knowledge and receive tailored advice based on their unique financial goals.

2. Goal Setting: Setting financial goals is a crucial step in achieving financial success. However, many students struggle to identify realistic and attainable goals. A financial advisor can assist in setting measurable goals and create a roadmap to achieve them. Whether it's saving for tuition, paying off student loans, or planning for the future, professional advice can provide clarity and direction.

3. Creating a Budget: Budgeting is an essential skill for students to develop early on. A financial advisor can help students create a personalized budget that aligns with their income, expenses, and

financial goals. They can provide valuable tips and strategies to manage spending, save for emergencies, and avoid unnecessary debt.

4. Investment Guidance: For students interested in investing, seeking professional advice is crucial. Financial advisors can educate students about various investment options, their risks, and potential returns. They can help students build a diversified investment portfolio that aligns with their risk tolerance and long-term financial goals.

5. Protection and Insurance: Insurance is another critical aspect of financial planning. Students need to protect themselves and their assets against unforeseen circumstances. Financial advisors can guide students in choosing the right insurance policies, such as health insurance, renters insurance, or auto insurance, ensuring they have adequate coverage without overspending.

In conclusion, seeking professional financial advice is a valuable step towards achieving financial success as a student. Financial advisors possess the knowledge, expertise, and tools to guide students in making informed decisions about their money. From setting financial goals to creating a budget, investing wisely, and protecting assets, their advice can make a significant difference in students' financial well-being. Remember, investing in professional guidance now can pave the way for a secure and prosperous financial future.

Continual Learning and Growth in Financial Literacy

In today's fast-paced and ever-changing world, financial literacy has become an essential skill for success. As students, you are embarking on a journey that will shape your future, and understanding how to manage your money effectively is crucial. In this subchapter, we will explore the concept of continual learning and growth in financial literacy, and how it can pave the way towards financial success.

Financial literacy is not a one-time achievement, but an ongoing process. It involves acquiring knowledge, developing skills, and cultivating the right mindset to make informed financial decisions. Just as you strive to improve your academic skills, it is equally important to invest time and effort into expanding your financial knowledge.

The first step towards continual learning is to recognize that financial literacy is not limited to the classroom. It is a real-life skill that requires practical application. Engage in activities such as reading books, attending seminars, or participating in online courses that focus on personal finance and money management. These resources will provide you with valuable insights and strategies to enhance your financial literacy.

Moreover, seek out mentors or advisors who have achieved financial success. Learning from their experiences and gaining insights into their financial journey can provide you with invaluable guidance. Additionally, consider joining clubs or organizations related to finance, as they can offer networking opportunities and allow you to learn from like-minded individuals.

Another crucial aspect of continual learning in financial literacy is staying updated with the latest trends and developments in the financial world. Keep an eye on economic news, investment strategies, and changes in government policies that may impact your finances. By staying aware of these factors, you can adapt your financial decisions accordingly and stay ahead of the curve.

Lastly, understand that financial literacy is not solely about managing money; it is also about cultivating a mindset of growth and lifelong learning. Embrace a growth mindset, which encourages you to view challenges as opportunities for growth and improvement. Be open to learning from your mistakes and seek feedback to continually refine your financial decisions.

In conclusion, continual learning and growth in financial literacy are essential for achieving financial success. By investing time and effort in expanding your financial knowledge, seeking guidance from mentors, staying updated with the latest trends, and cultivating a growth mindset, you will be equipped with the tools to make informed financial decisions that can lead you towards a prosperous future. Remember, financial literacy is a lifelong journey, and the more you learn, the more you can achieve.

Conclusion: Mastering Your Money Journey

Congratulations! You have reached the end of this book, "Mastering Money: A Guide to Financial Literacy for College Students." By now, you have gained a wealth of knowledge and practical tips to help you navigate your money journey successfully. In this final subchapter, we will recap the key takeaways and leave you with some empowering thoughts to set you on the path to financial success.

Throughout this book, we have emphasized the importance of financial literacy in your college years. By mastering your money, you are setting yourself up for a future of financial freedom and success. You have learned about budgeting, saving, investing, and managing debt. These skills will serve as a strong foundation for your financial well-being.

One of the key lessons we hope you take away from this book is the importance of setting financial goals. By defining your goals, whether it's paying off student loans, buying a car, or saving for a down payment on a house, you can create a roadmap to success. Remember, goals should be specific, measurable, attainable, relevant, and time-bound (SMART). By setting SMART goals, you can stay motivated and track your progress.

Additionally, we have stressed the significance of budgeting. A budget is a powerful tool that helps you understand where your money is going and make conscious choices about your spending. By practicing responsible financial habits, such as tracking your expenses, prioritizing needs over wants, and living within your means, you can take control of your finances and avoid unnecessary debt.

Another crucial aspect of financial literacy is understanding the importance of saving and investing. By starting early and consistently contributing to your savings and investment accounts, you can take advantage of compound interest, which will help your money grow over time. We have discussed different investment options, such as stocks, bonds, and mutual funds, and the importance of diversifying your portfolio to mitigate risks.

Finally, managing debt is an essential skill to master. We have provided guidance on responsible borrowing, understanding interest rates, and strategies for paying off debt efficiently. By staying on top of your debt and making timely payments, you can maintain a good credit score, which will open up opportunities for future financial endeavors.

As you embark on your financial journey, remember that it is a lifelong learning process. Keep educating yourself, staying informed about current financial trends, and adapting to changing circumstances. Surround yourself with a supportive network of mentors, friends, and resources that can guide you along the way.

In conclusion, mastering your money is a crucial step towards achieving success in life. By implementing the principles outlined in this book, you are equipping yourself with the necessary tools to make informed financial decisions and build a strong financial foundation. Remember, financial literacy is not a destination but a continuous journey. So, embrace it, stay disciplined, and enjoy the rewards that come with being financially savvy. Here's to your future of financial success!

Milton Keynes UK
Ingram Content Group UK Ltd.
UKHW020929231123
433129UK00016B/869